P9-CJZ-905
pull

WITHDRAWN

EDGE BOOKS

SPORTS RECORDS

THE GREATEST
BASKETBALL
RECORDS

BY MATT DOEDEN

CONSULTANT:
Craig R. Coenen, PhD
Associate Professor of History
Mercer County Community College
West Windsor, New Jersey

Mankato, Minnesota

Edge Books are published by Capstone Press,
151 Good Counsel Drive, P.O. Box 669, Mankato, Minnesota 56002.
www.capstonepress.com

Library of Congress Cataloging-in-Publication Data
Doeden, Matt.
    The greatest basketball records / by Matt Doeden.
    p. cm. — (Edge books. Sports records)
    Summary: "Short stories and tables of statistics describe the history and greatest
records of the National Basketball Association" — Provided by publisher.
    Includes bibliographical references and index.
    ISBN-13: 978-1-4296-2006-2 (hardcover)
    ISBN-10: 1-4296-2006-4 (hardcover)
    1. Basketball — Miscellanea — Juvenile literature. 2. National Basketball
Association — Juvenile Literature I. Title. II. Series.
    GV885.1.D64 2009
    796.323 — dc22
                                                    2008002033

Editorial Credits
Aaron Sautter, editor; Bobbi J. Wyss, designer; Jo Miller, photo researcher

Photo Credits
© [2008] Jupiterimages Corporation, cover (middle right)
AP Images, 20; Beth A. Keiser, 16; Jack Smith, 26; Rick Bowmer, 12
Corbis/Bettmann, 22
Getty Images Inc./Focus on Sport, cover (bottom right); Hulton Archive/
    Ernest Sisto, 4; Mike Powell, 24; NBAE/Andrew D. Bernstein, 7, 10;
    NBAE/Jerry Wachter, 28; NBAE/John Betancourt, 18; NBAE/Nathaniel
    S. Butler, 8; NBAE/Walter Iooss, 14; Robert Riger, 6; WireImage/Al
    Messerschmidt Archive, cover (top left)
Shutterstock/Albo, cover (bottom left); Michael Shake, cover (top right)

Records in this book are current through the 2007–08 regular season.

1 2 3 4 5 6 13 12 11 10 09 08

TABLE of CONTENTS

CHAPTER 1

SHOOTING FOR A RECORD

LEARN ABOUT
- Wilt's 100
- The Shot Clock
- Today's NBA

Wilt Chamberlain (#13) was one of the most dominant players in NBA history.

It was March 2, 1962, in Hershey, Pennsylvania. Fans filled the seats to watch the Philadelphia Warriors play the New York Knicks. They had no idea that they were about to see NBA history. Warrior center Wilt Chamberlain was a scoring machine that night. He scored 41 points in the first half. The Warrior fans chanted, "Give it to Wilt!"

The Warriors did just that, and Chamberlain kept scoring. Soon, he passed his old NBA record of 78 points in a game. With just 46 seconds left, he hit a jump shot to make it an even 100. Chamberlain's huge game led the Warriors to a big win with a final score of 169-147. The fans stormed onto the court to celebrate with one of the NBA's all-time greats.

THE EMERGING NBA

In 1946, the Basketball Association of America and the National Basketball League each competed for the attention of basketball fans. By 1949, the two leagues joined together to form the National Basketball Association (NBA). After the merger, the small league grew quickly. Stars like George Mikan of the Minneapolis Lakers led the way. Soon, fans packed the stadiums for every game.

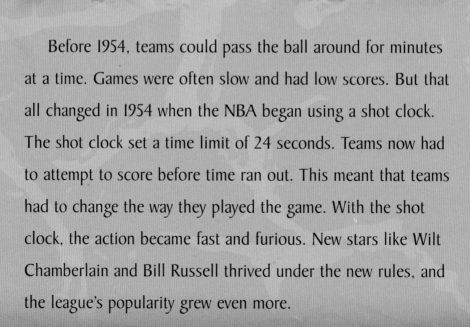

Before 1954, teams could pass the ball around for minutes at a time. Games were often slow and had low scores. But that all changed in 1954 when the NBA began using a shot clock. The shot clock set a time limit of 24 seconds. Teams now had to attempt to score before time ran out. This meant that teams had to change the way they played the game. With the shot clock, the action became fast and furious. New stars like Wilt Chamberlain and Bill Russell thrived under the new rules, and the league's popularity grew even more.

But it wasn't long before the NBA faced some strong competition. Beginning in 1967, the American Basketball Association (ABA) took many of the world's best players. But by 1976, the ABA was having money problems. In 1977, four teams from the ABA merged with the NBA to form the league as it is today. Since then, record-setting stars like Larry Bird, Earvin "Magic" Johnson, Michael Jordan, and Shaquille O'Neal have driven the NBA to great heights.

Magic Johnson (#32) and Larry Bird (#33) were strong rivals during the 1980s.

CHAPTER 2

BASKETBALL'S
GREATEST PLAYERS

LEARN ABOUT
- Scoring Champs
- Dominant Defenders
- Triple-Doubles

Many people feel that Michael Jordan (#23) is the greatest basketball player of all time.

8

A SCORING MACHINE

Nobody in NBA history has won more scoring titles than Michael Jordan. It didn't take long for the 6-foot, 6-inch (1.98 meter) Jordan to take the NBA by storm. During his rookie season in 1984, he averaged 28.2 points per game. It was just the beginning of an amazing career.

MOST SEASON SCORING TITLES

10	Michael Jordan	1987–93, 1996–98, Chicago
7	Wilt Chamberlain	1960–66, Philadelphia, San Francisco
4	George Gervin	1978–80, 1982, San Antonio
4	Allen Iverson	1999, 2001–02, 2005, Philadelphia

MOST TOTAL CAREER POINTS

38,387	Kareem Abdul-Jabbar	Milwaukee, Los Angeles
36,928	Karl Malone	Utah, Los Angeles
32,292	Michael Jordan	Chicago, Washington
31,419	Wilt Chamberlain	Philadelphia, San Francisco, Los Angeles, San Diego
27,409	Moses Malone	Buffalo, Houston, Philadelphia, Washington, Atlanta, Milwaukee, San Antonio

MOST POINTS IN A SINGLE GAME

100	Wilt Chamberlain	1962, vs. New York Knicks
81	Kobe Bryant	2006, vs. Toronto Raptors
78	Wilt Chamberlain	1961, vs. Los Angeles Lakers
73	Wilt Chamberlain	1962, vs. Chicago Zephyrs
73	Wilt Chamberlain	1962, vs. New York Knicks
73	David Thompson	1978, vs. Detroit Pistons

HIGHEST AVERAGE POINTS PER GAME IN A SEASON

50.4	Wilt Chamberlain	1961–62, Philadelphia Warriors
44.8	Wilt Chamberlain	1962–63, San Francisco Warriors
38.4	Wilt Chamberlain	1960–61, Philadelphia Warriors
38.3	Elgin Baylor	1961–62, Los Angeles Lakers
37.6	Wilt Chamberlain	1959–60, Philadelphia Warriors

Jordan was able to score from almost anywhere on the court. At times, he was nearly impossible to defend. His unique talents led him to a record 10 NBA scoring titles. Jordan was an even bigger star in the playoffs. His postseason heroics helped lead the Chicago Bulls to six NBA titles in the 1990s.

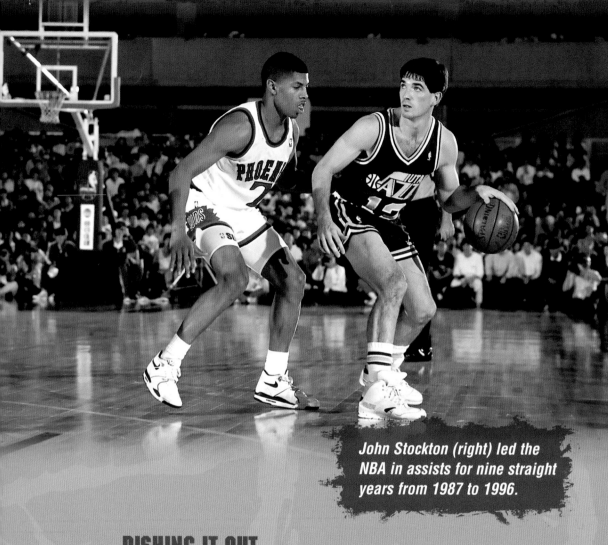

John Stockton (right) led the NBA in assists for nine straight years from 1987 to 1996.

DISHING IT OUT

When it comes to **assists**, John Stockton tops the list. During 19 NBA seasons, he dished out 15,806 of them. He led the league in assists nine times. This included the 1990–91 season, when he set the single-season record of 1,164 assists.

assist — a pass that leads to a score by a teammate

MOST ASSISTS IN A GAME

30	Scott Skiles	1990, Orlando Magic
29	Kevin Porter	1978, New Jersey Nets
28	Bob Cousy	1959, Boston Celtics
28	Guy Rodgers	1963, Philadelphia Warriors
28	John Stockton	1991, Utah Jazz

MOST ASSISTS IN A SEASON

1,164	John Stockton	1990–91, Utah Jazz
1,134	John Stockton	1989–90, Utah Jazz
1,128	John Stockton	1987–88, Utah Jazz
1,126	John Stockton	1991–92, Utah Jazz
1,123	Isiah Thomas	1984–85, Detroit Pistons

MOST CAREER ASSISTS

15,806	John Stockton	Utah
10,323	Mark Jackson	New York, L.A. Clippers, Indiana, Denver, Toronto, Utah, Houston
10,141	"Magic" Johnson	L.A. Lakers
9,887	Oscar Robertson	Cincinnati, Milwaukee
9,061	Isiah Thomas	Detroit

But Scott Skiles holds one assist record Stockton couldn't match. On December 30, 1990, the Orlando Magic guard was on fire against the Denver Nuggets. Late in the fourth quarter, he tied the single-game assist record at 29. With less than 20 seconds left in the game, he passed the ball to teammate Jerry Reynolds. Reynolds made the shot, and Skiles broke the assist record with 30.

Hakeem Olajuwon (#34) blocked more shots than any other NBA player.

PLAYING SOME "D"

NBA fans love watching offense. Dunks, three-pointers, and fast breaks are all thrilling plays. But defense is just as important. Great defensive players like Hakeem Olajuwon can change a game. Olajuwon used his 7-foot (2.13 meter) frame and long arms to swat away opposing shots. His 3,830 career **blocks** are an NBA record.

block — a defensive play made by swatting away the ball as it leaves an opponent's hands

MOST BLOCKS IN A GAME

17	Elmore Smith	1973, Los Angeles Lakers
15	Manute Bol	1986, Washington Bullets
15	Manute Bol	1987, Washington Bullets
15	Shaquille O'Neal	1993, Orlando Magic

MOST CAREER BLOCKS

3,830	Hakeem Olajuwon	Houston, Toronto
3,232	Dikembe Mutombo	Denver, Atlanta, Philadelphia, New Jersey, New York
3,189	Kareem Abdul-Jabbar	Milwaukee, L.A. Lakers
3,064	Mark Eaton	Utah
2,954	David Robinson	San Antonio

MOST STEALS IN A SEASON

301	Alvin Robertson	1985–86, San Antonio Spurs
281	Don Buse	1976–77, Indiana Pacers
265	Michael Ray Richardson	1979–80, New York Knicks
263	John Stockton	1988–89, Utah Jazz
261	Slick Watts	1975–76, Seattle Supersonics

MOST CAREER STEALS

3,265	John Stockton	Utah
2,514	Michael Jordan	Chicago, Washington
2,445	Gary Payton	Seattle, Milwaukee, L.A. Lakers, Boston, Miami
2,310	Maurice Cheeks	Philadelphia, San Antonio, New York, Atlanta, New Jersey
2,307	Scottie Pippen	Chicago, Houston, Portland

Other defenders work on stealing the ball. Nobody was better at that during the 1985–86 season than Alvin Robertson. Robertson's quick hands got him 301 steals that season — an average of 3.67 per game. His skills made him the all-time single-season steals leader.

Nobody has ever come close to matching Oscar Robertson's (#14) triple-double season.

THE TOTAL PACKAGE

The triple-double is one of the NBA's rarest feats. To get one, a player must reach double figures in points, rebounds, and assists in a game.

In the 1961–62 season, Cincinnati Royals guard Oscar Robertson made the triple-double look easy. With his smooth jump shots, accurate passes, and mastery of the ball, he was a major threat on the court. He finished the season averaging 30.8 points, 12.5 rebounds, and 11.4 assists per game. That means he averaged a triple-double over the entire season!

MOST CAREER TRIPLE-DOUBLE GAMES

181	Oscar Robertson	Cincinnati, Milwaukee
138	"Magic" Johnson	L.A. Lakers
87	Jason Kidd	Dallas, Phoenix, New Jersey
78	Wilt Chamberlain	Philadelphia, San Francisco, L.A. Lakers, San Diego
59	Larry Bird	Boston

MOST CAREER FREE THROW SHOTS MADE

9,787	Karl Malone	Utah, L.A. Lakers
8,531	Moses Malone	Buffalo, Houston, Philadelphia, Washington, Atlanta, Milwaukee, San Antonio
7,694	Oscar Robertson	Cincinnati, Milwaukee
7,327	Michael Jordan	Chicago, Washington
7,160	Jerry West	L.A. Lakers

MOST THREE-POINT SHOTS MADE IN A SEASON

269	Ray Allen	2005–06, Seattle SuperSonics
267	Dennis Scott	1995–96, Orlando Magic
257	George McCloud	1995–96, Dallas Mavericks
240	Peja Stojakovic	2003–04, Sacramento Kings
231	Mookie Blaylock	1995–96, Atlanta Hawks

HIGHEST THREE-POINT PERCENTAGE IN A SEASON

.524	Steve Kerr	1994–95, Chicago Bulls
.520	Tim Legler	1995–96, Washington Bullets
.515	Steve Kerr	1995–96, Chicago Bulls
.514	Jason Kapono	2006–07, Miami Heat
.514	Detlef Schrempf	1994–95, Seattle SuperSonics

EDGE FACT

No NBA player has appeared in more games than center Robert Parish. From 1976 to 1997, Parish played in 1,611 NBA games. He played for the Golden State Warriors, Boston Celtics, Charlotte Hornets, and Chicago Bulls.

CHAPTER 3

BASKETBALL'S
GREATEST TEAMS

LEARN ABOUT

- Legendary Teams
- Big-Time Scoring
- Winning it All

The Chicago Bulls were the most dominant NBA team of the 1990s.

Individual records get a lot of glory in the NBA. But basketball is a team game. Records are often broken when the best teams work together.

BEST WINNING PERCENTAGE IN A SEASON

.878 (72–10)	Chicago Bulls	1995–96
.841 (69–13)	Los Angeles Lakers	1971–72
.841 (69–13)	Chicago Bulls	1996–97
.840 (68–13)	Philadelphia 76ers	1966–67
.829 (68–14)	Boston Celtics	1972–73

LONGEST WINNING STREAKS

33 GAMES	Los Angeles Lakers	1971–72
22 GAMES	Houston Rockets	2008
20 GAMES	Milwaukee Bucks	1971
19 GAMES	Los Angeles Lakers	1999–00
18 GAMES	Boston Celtics	1982
18 GAMES	Chicago Bulls	1995–96
18 GAMES	New York Knicks	1969

BULLISH BEHAVIOR

The Chicago Bulls were the team to beat in the 1990s. Led by Michael Jordan and Scottie Pippen, the Bulls won six championship titles in that decade. Their best season was 1995–96. The team stormed out to an amazing 41-3 record to start the season. Then they cruised to the best season in NBA history. Their 72-10 mark and .878 winning percentage is the best the league has ever seen.

17

winning percentage — the number of games won divided by the number of games played

Alex English (#2) helped the Denver Nuggets become one of the highest scoring NBA teams of all time.

THE HIGH-FLYING NUGGETS

During the early 1980s, the Denver Nuggets were known for a great offense and a poor defense. The Nuggets' coach, Doug Moe, believed the best defense was a good offense. So the team ran up and down the court, shooting at will.

MOST TEAM POINTS IN A SEASON

10,371	Denver Nuggets	1981–82
10,147	Denver Nuggets	1983–84
10,143	Philadelphia 76ers	1966–67
10,105	Denver Nuggets	1982–83
10,051	Philadelphia 76ers	1967–68

MOST TEAM THREE-POINT SHOTS MADE IN A SEASON

837	Phoenix Suns	2005–06
796	Phoenix Suns	2004–05
785	Phoenix Suns	2006–07
735	Dallas Mavericks	1995–96
723	Seattle SuperSonics	2003–04

MOST TEAM FREE THROW SHOTS MADE IN A SEASON

2,434	Phoenix Suns	1969–70
2,408	Detroit Pistons	1960–61
2,388	Denver Nuggets	1980–81
2,378	Los Angeles Lakers	1961–62
2,371	Denver Nuggets	1981–82

Their unusual style resulted in lots of points, especially in the 1981–82 season. Alex English, Dan Issel, and Kiki Vandeweghe each averaged more than 20 points per game. The team scored a record 10,371 points, averaging 126.5 per game.

EDGE FACT

In 2001, Shaquille O'Neal and Kobe Bryant led the Los Angeles Lakers to a 15-1 playoff record on their way to the NBA title. It's the most dominant any team has ever been in the playoffs.

Bill Russell (#6) and coach Red Auerbach led the Boston Celtics to become the greatest team of the 1960s.

EIGHT STRAIGHT

Nobody wanted to face the Boston Celtics in the 1960s. Legendary coach Red Auerbach and Hall-of-Fame center Bill Russell led an almost unbeatable team. From 1957–1969, the Celtics won 11 of 13 possible titles.

During the 1968 and 1969 seasons, Bill Russell wasn't just the Celtics' best player — he also became the team's coach. Russell was the first African-American coach in any major sport to win a championship title.

MOST NBA CHAMPIONSHIPS

16	Boston Celtics	1957, 1959–66, 1968–69, 1974, 1976, 1981, 1984, 1986
14	Los Angeles Lakers	1949–50, 1952–54, 1972, 1980, 1982, 1985, 1987–88, 2000–02
6	Chicago Bulls	1991–93, 1996–98
4	San Antonio Spurs	1999, 2003, 2005, 2007
3	Detroit Pistons	1989–90, 2004

MOST CONSECUTIVE NBA CHAMPIONSHIPS

8	Boston Celtics	1959–66
3	Minneapolis Lakers	1952–54
3	Chicago Bulls	1991–93
3	Chicago Bulls	1996–98
3	Los Angeles Lakers	2000–02

The Celtics also hold the record for consecutive championships. From 1959 to 1966, the Celtics won eight straight NBA titles. That's not just an NBA record. It's also a record for all major pro sports. The Celtics' total of 16 NBA championships is also a record. Only the Los Angeles Lakers, at 14 titles, are even close.

EDGE FACT

In the 1985–86 season, the Boston Celtics were almost perfect at home. They went 40-1 in the Boston Garden to post the best home record in NBA history.

CHAPTER 4

BASKETBALL'S WILDEST RECORDS

LEARN ABOUT

- A Record Game
- Playing Injured
- Size Differences

On December 13, 1983, fans were treated to a record 370 total points between the Nuggets and the Pistons.

22

The NBA record book isn't just about career milestones. The strange and unexpected are also a big part of what makes the game so popular.

MOST COMBINED POINTS IN A GAME

370	Detroit Pistons, 186 vs. Denver Nuggets, 184	1983
337	San Antonio Spurs, 171 vs. Milwaukee Bucks, 166	1982
320	Golden State Warriors, 162 vs. Denver Nuggets, 158	1990
318	Denver Nuggets, 163 vs. San Antonio Spurs, 155	1984
318	Phoenix Suns, 161 vs. New Jersey Nets, 157	2006

370 POINTS

Most NBA teams have a great shot at winning if they score 100 points. But on December 13, 1983, the Detroit Pistons needed a lot more than that. The Pistons were locked in a high-scoring battle with the Denver Nuggets. Isiah Thomas, Kelly Tripucka, and Kiki Vandeweghe were making baskets all night long.

At the end of regulation time, the teams were tied 145-145. After two overtimes, the game was knotted at 171. Detroit finally finished off the Nuggets after three overtimes. Detroit's final total of 186 points is an NBA record. Denver scored 184, the second most in history. Their combined total of 370 points will be tough to beat.

23

EDGE FACT

The NBA's longest game took place on January 6, 1951. After an incredible six overtimes, the Indianapolis Olympians finally beat the Rochester Royals 75-73.

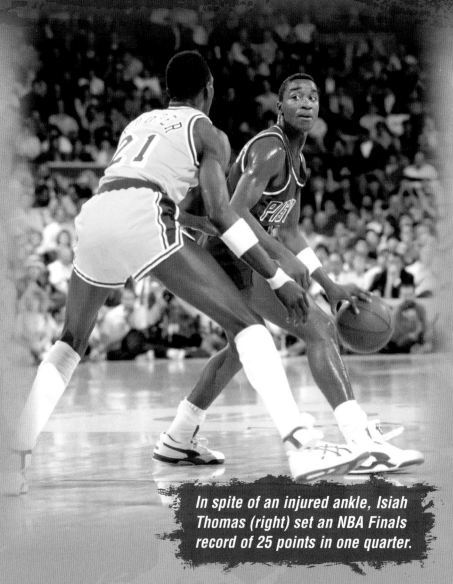

In spite of an injured ankle, Isiah Thomas (right) set an NBA Finals record of 25 points in one quarter.

25 ON A BUM ANKLE

It was June 19, 1988. The Pistons and Lakers were battling in game six of the NBA Finals. Pistons point guard Isiah Thomas got a hot start in the third quarter. But then he twisted his ankle when landing from a jump. He had to be helped off the court.

MOST CAREER POINTS IN PLAYOFFS

5,987	Michael Jordan	Chicago, Washington
5,762	Kareem Abdul-Jabbar	Milwaukee, L.A. Lakers
5,045	Shaquille O'Neal	Orlando, L.A. Lakers, Miami, Phoenix
4,761	Karl Malone	Utah, L.A. Lakers
4,457	Jerry West	L.A. Lakers

MOST POINTS IN A PLAYOFF GAME

63	Michael Jordan	April 20, 1986, vs. Boston Celtics
61	Elgin Baylor	April 14, 1962, vs. Boston Celtics
56	Wilt Chamberlain	March 22, 1962, vs. Syracuse Nationals
56	Michael Jordan	April 29, 1992, vs. Miami Heat
56	Charles Barkley	May 4, 1994, vs. Golden State Warriors

Less than a minute later, Thomas was back. He had a bad limp, but that didn't stop him. He made shot after shot, scoring a Finals record of 25 points in one quarter. Thomas' gutsy performance wasn't enough for the Pistons, though. They lost the game 103-102.

25

EDGE FACT

On November 25, 1977, the Milwaukee Bucks trailed the Atlanta Hawks by 29 points with less than nine minutes left to play. But the Bucks outscored the Hawks 35-4 down the stretch. It was the biggest comeback in NBA history.

Rasheed Wallace's bad bahavior resulted in seven ejections in the 2000–01 season.

UNWANTED RECORDS

Not all NBA records are something to brag about. Consider the record Rasheed Wallace set in 2000–01. The Portland Trail Blazers forward racked up 41 **technical fouls** for bad behavior. On top of that, his behavior got him ejected from seven games that season too.

technical foul — a foul called for unsportsmanlike behavior

WORST WINNING PERCENTAGE IN A SEASON

.110	(9-73)	Philadelphia 76ers	1972–73
.125	(6-42)	Providence Steamrollers	1947–48
.134	(11-71)	Dallas Mavericks	1992–93
.134	(11-71)	Denver Nuggets	1997–98
.146	(12-70)	Los Angeles Clippers	1986–87

MOST TURNOVERS IN A SEASON

366	Artis Gilmore	1977–78, Chicago Bulls
360	Kevin Porter	1977–78, Detroit Pistons/New Jersey Nets
359	Michael Ray Richardson	1979–80, New York Knicks
352	Ricky Sobers	1977–78, Indiana Pacers
350	Charles Barkley	1985–86, Philadelphia 76ers

UNWANTED PLAYER RECORDS

4,657	Most personal fouls in a career:	Kareem Abdul-Jabbar	1969–89
386	Most personal fouls in a season:	Darryl Dawkins	1983–84
4,524	Most turnovers in a career:	Karl Malone	1985–2004
14	Most turnovers in a game:	John Drew	1978
		and Jason Kidd	2000

Sometimes entire teams hit low points. On April 10, 1999,
the Chicago Bulls scored just 49 points in the whole game.
It's the lowest total since the NBA added the shot clock in 1954.
Plus, both the Dallas Mavericks and the Golden State Warriors
have managed to score just 2 points in an entire quarter!

EDGE FACT

The lowest-scoring game in NBA history came on
November 22, 1950. In this pre-shot-clock game, the
Fort Wayne Pistons beat the Minneapolis Lakers by
the low score of 19-18.

Manute Bol (left) and "Muggsy" Bogues (right) both played for the Washington Bullets in the 1987–88 season.

TALLEST NBA PLAYERS

7 FEET, 7 INCHES (2.31 METERS)	Manute Bol
7 FEET, 7 INCHES (2.31 METERS)	Gheorghe Muresan
7 FEET, 6 INCHES (2.28 METERS)	Shawn Bradley
7 FEET, 6 INCHES (2.28 METERS)	Yao Ming

SHORTEST NBA PLAYERS

5 FEET, 3 INCHES (1.60 METERS)	Tyrone "Muggsy" Bogues
5 FEET, 5 INCHES (1.65 METERS)	Earl Boykins
5 FEET, 7 INCHES (1.70 METERS)	Anthony "Spud" Webb

TALL AND SHORT

Height is a big advantage in the NBA. But who were the game's tallest players? Manute Bol and Gheorghe Muresan share that honor. They each stood a dizzying 7 feet, 7 inches (2.31 meters) tall. Bol was a shot-blocking machine from 1985 to 1995. Muresan's career lasted from 1993 to 2005.

Who was the shortest player? Tyrone "Muggsy" Bogues stood just 5 feet, 3 inches (1.60 meters) tall. Teammates and opponents towered over the little point guard. But that didn't stop Bogues. He enjoyed a successful NBA career from 1987 to 2001.

Basketball is a game packed with action. Fans love watching high-flying dunks, pinpoint passes, and three-point bombs. With all the fast-paced action, fans never know when a new record will be set to rewrite NBA history.

29

GLOSSARY

assist (uh-SIST) — a pass that leads to a score by a teammate

block (BLOK) — a defensive play made by swatting away the ball as it leaves an opponent's hands

consecutive (kuhn-SEK-yuh-tiv) — when something happens several times in a row without a break

personal foul (PUR-suh-nuhl FOUL) — a foul called for illegal physical contact

rebound (REE-bound) — to take possession of the ball after it bounces off the backboard or rim

shot clock (SHOT KLOK) — a clock that limits teams to 24 seconds to take a shot at the basket

technical foul (TEK-nuh-kuhl FOUL) — a foul called for unsportsmanlike behavior

triple-double (trip-uhl-DUH-buhl) — an achievement made when a player reaches double digits in points, assists, and rebounds

winning percentage (WIN-ing pur-SEN-tij) — the number of games won divided by the number of games played

READ MORE

Giglio, Joe. *Great Teams in Pro Basketball History.* Great Teams. Chicago: Raintree, 2006.

LeBoutillier, Nate. *The Story of the Boston Celtics.* The NBA: A History of Hoops. North Mankato, Minn.: Creative Education, 2007.

Stewart, Mark. *The NBA Finals.* The Watts History of Sports. New York: Franklin Watts, 2003.

INTERNET SITES

FactHound offers a safe, fun way to find Internet sites related to this book. All of the sites on FactHound have been researched by our staff.

Here's how:
1. Visit *www.facthound.com*
2. Choose your grade level.
3. Type in this book ID **1429620064** for age-appropriate sites. You may also browse subjects by clicking on letters, or by clicking on pictures and words.
4. Click on the **Fetch It** button.

FactHound will fetch the best sites for you!

INDEX